Paper

Sally Morgan and Pauline Lalor

WHY WASTE IT?

SIMON & SCHUSTER
YOUNG BOOKS

The authors wish to thank The Dover Fine Paper Mill
of Arjo-Wiggins-Appleton plc
for their advice on this project.

WHY WASTE IT? has been researched and compiled by
Simon & Schuster Young Books.   We are very
grateful for the support and guidance provided
by our advisory panel of professional
educationalists in the course of the production.

Advisory panel:
Colin Pidgeon, Headteacher
Wheatfields Junior School, St Albans
Deirdre Walker, Deputy headteacher
Wheatfields Junior School, St Albans
Judith Clarke, Headteacher
Grove Infants School, Harpenden

Commissioning editor: Daphne Butler
Book editor: Claire Llewellyn
Design: M&M Design Partnership
Photographs: Ecoscene except for
page 7 Zefa.

First published in Great Britain in 1992
by Simon & Schuster Young Books

Simon & Schuster Young Books
Campus 400, Maylands Avenue
Hemel Hempstead, Herts HP2 7EZ

A catalogue record for this book
is available from the British Library
ISBN 0 7500 1092 4

Printed and bound in Great Britain
by BPCC Hazell Books, Paulton and
Aylesbury

Contents

We use paper in many ways

Paper comes in all sorts of sizes,
colours, shapes and thicknesses.
It has dozens of different uses.
How many can you spot in the picture?
How else do we use paper?

Most paper is made from trees

Paper can be made from most types of plants.   Today most of our paper is made from conifers, which grow very fast and straight.

The trees are grown in special forests called plantations.   When they are cut down, more trees are planted so that more paper can be made.

Paper is made in a paper mill

The huge logs are chopped up into small pieces.   Lots of water and some chemicals are added to make a mixture which is like wet cotton wool.

The mixture is spread onto a moving belt. The water drains away through tiny holes, leaving a long sheet of wet paper.

A4 WEBS
ONLY

NOTICE

Drying the wet paper

The long wet sheet is rolled flat and dried on hot rollers.   It is then wound onto huge reels.   The heat makes the paper mill very warm.

Before we can buy the paper, it has to be cut up into sheets by machines and packed in boxes.

How large are the sheets of paper you use at home and at school?

Different kinds of paper

Paper which is strong and thick is often made into cardboard for boxes.

Paper which is soft and easily torn is just right for tissue paper or kitchen rolls.

Have you ever looked at paper through a magnifying glass?   Tear some and look at the edge.   Are all types of paper the same?

Paper for printing and writing

Most paper is used for printing books and newspapers, or for writing and drawing.

Not all paper is good enough to write on.   What happens when you write on soft paper with a felt-tip pen?

We throw away too much paper

Every day we throw away newspapers, magazines, bags, letters, cardboard boxes – all made from paper.

Some of this waste paper can be used again to make new paper.   This is called recycling.

Collecting waste paper

In some towns, newspapers and magazines for recycling are collected from homes.

Other towns have special collection points, called paper banks, where people can take their waste paper.

Do you know what happens in your town?

Recycling waste paper

Waste paper is taken to the paper mill in huge bales.   The bales are shredded and mixed with water and chemicals.

Recycled paper is not as good as the paper which is made from trees.
What could it be used for?

New paper from old

Paper bags, cardboard boxes and toilet
rolls are just a few things which
can be made from recycled paper.

When you go shopping, how can you tell
whether something has been made with
recycled paper?

Recycling saves water

Huge amounts of water are needed to
turn a tree into paper.   Much less
is needed to make recycled paper.

Saving water is important.   Think what
would happen if we ran out of it.
How could you save water?

Recycling saves the countryside

Have you ever walked through a forest of conifers?   They are cold, dark places, and few animals make their homes there.

If we recycle plenty of paper, we won't need to plant as many fir plantations.   This will help wildlife. Can you think why?

Index